Catch That Chicken!

Archie has stolen Charlie's prize hat – the race is on to get it back. Catch that chicken!

This picture book targets the /ch/ sound and is part of *Speech Bubbles 2*, a series of picture books that target specific speech sounds within the story.

The series can be used for children receiving speech therapy, for children who have a speech sound delay/disorder, or simply as an activity for children's speech sound development and/or phonological awareness. They are ideal for use by parents, teachers or caregivers.

Bright pictures and a fun story create an engaging activity perfect for sound awareness.

Picture books are sold individually, or in a pack. There are currently two packs available – *Speech Bubbles 1* and *Speech Bubbles 2.* Please see further titles in the series for stories targeting other speech sounds.

Melissa Palmer is a Speech Language Therapist. She worked for the Ministry of Education, Special Education in New Zealand from 2008 to 2013, with children aged primarily between 2 and 8 years of age. She also completed a diploma in children's writing in 2009, studying under author Janice Marriott, through the New Zealand Business Institute. Melissa has a passion for articulation and phonology, as well as writing and art, and has combined these two loves to create *Speech Bubbles*.

T0143527

What's in the pack?

User Guide

Vinnie the Dove

Rick's Carrot

Harry the Hopper

Have You Ever Met a Yeti?

Zack the Buzzy Bee

Asher the Thresher Shark

Catch That Chicken!

Will the Wolf

Magic Licking Lollipops

Jasper the Badger

Platypus and Fly

The Dragon Drawing War

Catch That Chicken!

Chicken!

Targeting the /ch/ Sound

Melissa Palmer

Routledge
Taylor & Francis Group

LONDON AND NEW YORK

First published 2021
by Routledge
2 Park Square, Milton Park, Abingdon, Oxon OX14 4RN

and by Routledge
52 Vanderbilt Avenue, New York, NY 10017

Routledge is an imprint of the Taylor & Francis Group, an informa business

British Library Cataloguing-in-Publication Data
A catalogue record for this book is available from the British Library

Library of Congress Cataloging-in-Publication Data
A catalog record has been requested for this book

ISBN: 978-1-138-59784-6 (set)
ISBN: 978-0-367-64875-6 (pbk)
ISBN: 978-1-003-12671-3 (ebk)

Typeset in Calibri
by Newgen Publishing UK

Catch That Chicken!

Charlie the Ostri**ch** **ch**erished his hat. He **ch**ose to wear it morning, noon and night. It had a pat**ch** on the front with **ch**erries on it, whi**ch** he loved.

One day while **Ch**arlie munched on some spina**ch** in the yard, Ar**ch**ie the **ch**icken was pecking around his feet, sear**ch**ing for food. **Ch**arlie looked down to **ch**eck on the **ch**icken ...

... and his hat fell off ...

… straight onto Ar**ch**ie!

The **ch**erry hat was far too big for poor Ar**ch**ie, and he couldn't see! **Ch**eeping in panic, he **ch**arged off blindly, taking **Ch**arlie's hat with him.

"My hat!" yelled **Ch**arlie. "Cat**ch** that **ch**icken!"

Charlie chased Archie across the yard. Archie fell into a mud patch and was covered in sticky mud, but he still didn't stop.

"Catch that chicken!" Charlie yelled.

Ar**ch**ie **ch**arged onto a picnic lunch, spread out on a blanket at the bea**ch**. He stomped on a platter of crunchy na**ch**o **ch**ips, whi**ch** stuck to the mud, stuck on Ar**ch**ie.

"Cat**ch** that **ch**icken!" **Ch**arlie yelled.

Ar**ch**ie crashed into a plate of grated **ch**eese, whi**ch** stuck to the mud.

"Cat**ch** that **ch**icken!"

Ar**ch**ie fell onto a bowl of **ch**ocolate **ch**ips, whi**ch** also stuck to the mud. He still couldn't see, and lurched off the blanket through the sand, and straight into the ocean.

"Cat**ch** that **ch**icken!"

The water washed the na**ch**os, **ch**eese and **ch**ocolate **ch**ips away, but the **ch**erry hat still stayed on his head. Poor Ar**ch**ie still couldn't see, and his beak started to **ch**atter with the cold **-ch-ch-ch-ch-ch-ch-ch-ch-ch-ch-**

Suddenly, Ar**ch**ie was pulled out of the **ch**illy water, and the hat was pinched off his head. He could see! He looked up into **Ch**arlie's face.

"Thanks **Ch**arlie, you saved me!" Ar**ch**ie said, his beak still **ch**attering.

Charlie rea**ch**ed down and clut**ch**ed Ar**ch**ie close to him to warm him up.

"You're welcome, Ar**ch**ie. I just wanted my **ch**erry hat back. It doesn't fit your head, but it fits me perfectly."

"Well … let's go back and eat that picnic lunch – there's no one to cat**ch** us!"

So they quickly went and ate the rest of the na**ch**os, the **ch**ocolate **ch**ips and the **ch**eese. There was even a pit**ch**er of pea**ch** juice, whi**ch** they **ch**ugged quickly.

They snuck away when they heard some **ch**ildren coming.

The **ch**ildren scratched their heads confused – they would never have guessed that an ostri**ch** and a **ch**icken would steal their lunch!